Speak Up,
Child,
and Be Saved

Speak Up, Child, and Be Saved

By Tyrone Short

Xulon Press Elite

Xulon Press Elite
2301 Lucien Way #415
Maitland, FL 32751
407.339.4217
www.xulonpress.com

E xulon LITE

Unless otherwise indicated, Scripture quotations taken
from the HOLY BIBLE, New International Version (NIV).
Copyright © 1973, 1978, 1984, 2011 by Biblica, Inc.™.
Used by permission. All rights reserved.

Printed in the United States of America.

ISBN-13: 9781545647707

Whether you are a victim of sexual abuse or domestic violence, keeping it to yourself does more harm than good for many reasons. What happened to you should have never happened, and as much as it hurt you at the time, the ramifications for not speaking up can be even more hurtful.

This man will pay for what he did whether you speak up or not, so speaking up is not for him; it is for you. Not only is it for you, but it is for your family and for your loved ones as well. It is also for your future relationship with them.

Bad things happen in this world, and some things are more devastating than others. However, there is a difference between a guy messing up your night or weekend and a guy being allowed to mess up your life.

Therefore, speak up, Child, and be saved.

Table of Contents

---⟋🙢⟍---

I divorced my wife in 2001. Shortly thereafter, I found myself back on the dating scene, where I had the pleasure of meeting a very special lady, who, for obvious reasons, will remain nameless. This woman was such a sweet person; however, there was an obvious sense of shyness and reservation within her, more than I was familiar with. We went on a couple of dates prior to me initiating our first kiss. Respectfully, the kiss was awkward, to say the least.

As I attempted to kiss her after coming out of a movie theatre, she had the look of a "deer in headlights." Even though I saw this look as I was going forward, I continued to dive in with the kiss. At first, she moved her head back, but then she brought her head back so that I could kiss her. She immediately started smiling and blushing, and then she started giggling. This was not the response I expected, so I had asked her if everything was okay. She stated that she was okay and apologized for the response. She then said she had to share something with me. She said that normally she doesn't allow anyone to kiss her so quickly without getting to know them a little better, but she said that I seemed like a nice guy, so she was okay with it. Then, she said one of the most profound things I have ever heard — something that has played in my head for years for many reasons.

She said: "I have to tell you something before we go any further. When I was a child, I was sexually molested by a family relative."

"Oh my gosh, I'm so sorry," I responded.

"It's okay. I have moved on."

I then asked her, "Was the person ever arrested?" She said that he wasn't, so I asked why not.

"Because I didn't tell anyone," she said. "Because no one would have believed me."

As we continued our conversation, she revealed that this man was her uncle. She then shared with me the poor relationship she had with her mother, which was one of the reasons that she decided not to tell her. She shared the pain and anguish she had to endure for years thinking about what this man did to her. She also shared that I was the first person that she ever told this to. This was so disheartening, because she stated that this happened to her when she was about eight. When we had this conversation, she was about thirty-eight.

This should not happen. This should not be. No child should be left alone to deal with the tragedy of being sexually molested. No child should be left alone to deal with the emotional and physical scars of being sexually molested. No child should be left alone.

Speak up, Child, and be saved.

**** Not every scenario written in this book will match what may have happened to you; however, they had to be written because they were reality for other victims I have met and may be for others who will read this book. Since some readers may be able to relate to these stories, these testimonies may just be enough for readers to speak up.

Also, I do warn that some of the contents in this book may trigger painful memories of the past for anyone who was or is a victim of sexual abuse. However, my goal is to push, incite, and inspire you to speak up against the monster who violated you.

Train Up a Child in the Way She Should Go

It is a parent's job to train his or her child in things pertaining to life issues; it is not the responsibility of the schools. The schools teach the child academics, which is their primary responsibility. It is the parents' responsibility to teach the kids life lessons such as how to share, how to get along with others, how to say please and thank you, the difference between right and wrong, and how to speak up.

It is a parent's job to teach his or her child to speak up when something doesn't feel right. It is the parent's job to teach his or her child to speak up when he or she feels they are being wronged. It is a parent's job to teach his or her child to speak up when the child has been violated.

A parent can't rely on the schools to teach the child the valuable lessons, because it may be too late, for these types of violations may happen at school.

The authorities at the school are not going to cry out for your child when she comes home with her clothing ripped. The authorities at the school are not going to stay up late comforting your child while she is up crying and screaming that night. The authorities at the school are not going to sit with your daughter at a clinic as she is tested for pregnancy and sexually transmitted diseases, while she sits there shaking, crying, and fearing the worst. The authorities at the school will not be there, but you will, for you are the parent.

Therefore, train the child. Train the child how to avoid being alone and being that lone, lost sheep, thus making her an easy target. Train the child how to scream and fight her way out of a situation, for it may hurt if the predator were to fight back, but it will hurt more if he were to get her where he wants her and have his way with her. Train the child to speak up if all else fails and she becomes victim to someone that molests her.

There is an old saying: "There is never a problem, until there is a problem." In many cases of molestation, this saying is something that reflected the ideology of many parents, because the question by outsiders that will follow a molestation is, "Why did she leave her daughter with that man in the first place?"

This question follows because, in many cases, the mother may have been involved with a convicted molester and had hoped for the best when leaving her child with him. However, when her worst fear comes to reality and she is questioned for her poor choice, one of things that she will say is, "it was never a problem when I left her with him before." There is never a problem, until there is a problem.

If you are a parent, train your child. Don't wait until something happens before you recognize your failure to prepare her. If you are a parent, train your child, so she can have a fighting chance of getting out unscathed. If you are a parent, train your child. Don't be naïve and think it could never happen to your child. If you are a parent, train your child. Don't wait until you have to witness your child cowering in a corner of her bedroom crying upon your return home, and before she could say anything, the first thought that came to your mind was that you just saw your boyfriend or babysitter leaving abruptly. Train your child.

Train your child to speak up so that she can be saved.

Expose Him

———————— ✎ ————————

There is a man who is lurking and searching. He is searching for a victim. He is searching for someone to take advantage of. He is searching for a child.

He is searching for a child because he is weak. He is a coward. He is filled with a demonic perverseness and has allowed his evil desires to control him. Thus, he has become an enemy of God. And one day he will have to face an angry God, but until then:

"Have nothing to do with the fruitless deeds of darkness, but rather expose them" (Ephesians 5:11).

This cowardly, perverted, evil man forced you to participate in this dark and evil act. Well, now God has a command for you; expose him!

Expose him; let his shame and guilt be known to those around him. Expose him; rescue others from being ensnared by this man's snatch. Expose him; let it be a deterrent to others who would walk in his ways. Expose him, so you can have peace and closure in this matter.

You will not have peace until you have closure in this area. You will not have peace if this man is still walking in your circle, walking in your neighborhood, and heaven forbid, in your household. Your home should be your safe haven; you should never be at unrest and scared of anyone who dwells in your home. Therefore, if this man dwells in your house, and you feel uncomfortable telling anyone else that lives there, then tell a neighbor; tell a teacher, but tell someone. So, whether this man is a stranger, a relative, or your mother's boyfriend, you will have no peace if you have to see him daily or even once in a while, as he smiles at you cynically, as if to say, "This is our little secret."

How dare he? How dare he smile at you as if the two of you are in some covenant? How dare he blatantly make a mockery of you and the transgression that you suffered at his hands?

Speak up and expose him!

You need peace; therefore, expose him and wipe that smile off of his face. You need peace;

therefore, expose him and instill the fear in him that he once placed in you. You need peace; therefore, expose him because it is his turn to cry out for mercy, as you once did.

Speak up, Child. Expose him and be saved.

Be Saved

What this man did has the ability to affect you for the rest of your life. Also, what this man did to you can affect every aspect of your life, if you allow it. This is why it is important for you to speak up immediately after the first offense.

An analogy that can be used is this: if you were to mistakenly place your hand on a flame, the quicker you move it away, the less chance there is for long-term injury. If you were to move your hand away immediately, it is possible you could stick your hand under cold running water and be fine. However, if you allowed it to sit on the flame for a while, the result could be life-threatening, to the point that you will never be able to use it again.

It is the same in regards to being sexually molested; the longer that you allow it to go on, the more likely that you will face life-sustaining injuries, emotional and physical.

When a child is molested, even if it was just a one-time incident, it will not be something easily forgotten after a couple of days. A molested child can be psychologically affected for the rest of her life.

A molested child can be traumatized for life, and the trauma can affect her future relationships with the opposite sex to the point that they become unhealthy. They can become unhealthy in the aspect that the child can become promiscuous, or she can develop an unhealthy fear of men altogether.

The trauma can also affect her relationships with family members in the sense that she develops a lack of trust and does not believe her family is reliable when bad situations come about, for she may feel subconsciously that they let her down, even if they did not know that the incident had even occurred. The trauma can also affect her parenting skills, as she may develop an unhealthy protectiveness toward her children to the point that she can't even trust her own husband around their child, no matter how much of a decent man he is. Or even worse, she can become callous in regards to the safety of her kids to the degree that she feels that because she had to endure being molested, her child will have to figure out on her own how to deal with the trauma and survive.

For reasons such as this, the quicker a molested child speaks up, the better the chances of recovery are.

Speak up, Child, and be saved from living with any of these ramifications.

Saved from Further Abuse

---❦---

There is a phrase which goes, "nip it in the bud." This phrase basically means to stop a potential problem before it develops into something bigger. In the case of sexual molestation, the hope is that the victim is able to stop the potential problem before it develops by telling a parent, "He makes me feel uncomfortable," or if the perpetrator is the father, the child speak up and tell a teacher or another adult.

Unfortunately, this doesn't always happen. When it does, on many occasions, I believe the child might be brushed off. When this occurs, if you are a child in this stage, I plead with you to continue to speak up until someone listens. Speak up, and tell a neighbor. Tell a pastor at a church. Tell a policeman. Tell a fireman. Tell a teacher. Speak up, and nip it in the bud.

However, if we are past that stage and the event has occurred, you have even more reason to speak up. Speak up to be saved from further abuse.

Further abuse is when this man is allowed to continue to use you as his object to relieve himself. Further abuse is when this man is allowed to continue to bring shame to you. Further abuse is when this man is allowed to continue to terrorize you.

It is easier for you to get over it and move on after having to endure just one bad event opposed to a series of bad events. It is easier for you to speak up after having experienced a single horrible experience than it is for you to speak up after having to deal with a horrible experience you endure for months and almost become "used to" being in that situation—the initial traumatic shock is gone. It would be easier for you to speak up after just having experienced a horrible experience, when you are angry, disgusted, freaked out, and even more filled with an overwhelming passion to get revenge on this man, as opposed to when this situation has gone on for quite some time and the tears are gone, the pain is no more, and you have become hardened and have learned to accept it.

Cry, Child. Let it all out, and then speak up. Remember the pain that he put you through. This alone should entice you to want to expose him. Moreover, do not allow yourself to get used to it; be saved from this position.

Speak up, Child, and be saved.

Saved from the Guilt and Shame of Not Speaking Up

---- ❧ ----

Child, if you don't speak up, you will regret it. Your silence will haunt you forever. Lack of speaking up will tear into your inner soul.

You will always wonder what would have had happened had you spoke up. You will wonder if justice would have ever been served. You will wonder if the anxious thoughts that go through your head today would have been a thing of the past. You will wonder if the many failed relationships you have had since the encounter with this man took place were a result of his hold, control, and the bondage he had over you.

Speak up, so that you will not have to lie in bed regularly and wonder how many people you have let down because you didn't speak up. Speak up, so that you will not have to lie in bed regularly and wonder if he is doing this now to someone else. Speak up, so that your guilt will go away.

Along with this guilt will come shame — a shame of yourself for not speaking up, a shame so powerful that it will feel like hot flashes every time you recall the incident. You will feel that shame every time someone brings up the perpetrator's name, and you are still holding that secret to yourself. You will feel that shame every time you hear of a child elsewhere being molested. You will feel that shame when you hear (heaven forbid) that your perpetrator is suspected of having molested another child after you. When you hear this, you will be ashamed that you didn't speak up.

You will be ashamed because you will know in your heart that you could have possibly prevented this. You will be ashamed because you will know in your heart that you had a responsibility to let those around you know that this man was not right. You will be ashamed because you will know in your heart that you did not inform the community that there was a monster loose amongst them.

As long as you live with this guilt, you will never have peace. As long as you never have peace, you will never be able to properly function in society. You will have good days, but when the memory of what once occurred engulfs you, you will be back in your depressed state.

There are many who walk through life living with depression. Why should you be one of them? Why should you walk around life being depressed because of something that wasn't your fault? You will be depressed at school, at work, at home, around your family, around your friends. Your depression will be evident in your moodiness. You will be up one moment and then not feeling like being bothered the next.

Why allow yourself to live a life of feeling guilty when all you had to do was say, ***"That man touched me!"***

If you speak up, the guilt that comes from not speaking up will be turned into joy. Joy comes because you know you saved yourself from a life of guilt. It will be the joy of knowing that you had the strength and courage to speak up and do what was right.

Speak up, so you will not have to live in secret, afraid to talk about what happened to you. Speak up, so you will not have to live without peace because you did not expose him. Speak up, so you will not have to live in guilt because you just wanted it to all go away, and it didn't.

Speak up, Child, and be saved.

Saved from Paranoia

—————— ❧ ——————

There are good men out there, and unfortunately, there are bad men. Bad men do things
that make it hard for good women to trust all men.

Bad men cheat on their mates, which in turn
develops a sense of distrust that their mates bring
into future relationships. Bad men don't know
how to control their temper, and hit their mates,
which in turn develops a sense of fear that their
mates bring into future relationships. Bad men
molest little girls, and those little girls have to live
with this violation all their lives, which in turn
develops a sense of paranoia toward many future
male relationships. This includes male friends,
male family members, and, of course, possible
boyfriends.

When a child is molested, it is possible that she
may see every adult male in her life as a potential

threat. Unfortunately, for some, they are placed in positions where they have a reason to be concerned. This would be to the shame of many parents who daily place their children in jeopardy by leaving them in the care of unsavory characters.

My heart goes out to the child who was molested by one of her mother's boyfriends, then, within a year, was molested by another one of her mother's boyfriends, or worse, a family member in the same house. In such a house as this, the child needs to speak up to someone on the outside, as this is an unsafe environment.

Speak up, Child. Let someone know that you don't feel safe at home.

Speak up, Child. Let someone know that you have been molested at home.

Speak up, Child. Let someone know that you don't trust your mother's judgement anymore.

Why should you grow up and no longer trust men and be paranoid that they all might be out to abuse you in some way? There are good men out there who, if they knew of your plight, would be just as distraught and willing to help you as someone who is a parent to you.

19

Therefore, do not shun or view every man who comes across your life as a potential threat. Instead, see to it that the one responsible for the trespass is exposed and held accountable, and you will see how good men will play a role in prosecuting this monster.

Therefore, do not allow paranoia to overwhelm you if you are a single parent. Do not get to the point that you chase away every man that comes into your life with suspicions or accusations that he may be or is planning to molest your child. This man may be the blessing that you have been praying for.

Instead, instruct and train your child to spot the red flags. Teach your child to speak up if someone is getting too close and paying too much attention to her to the point that she feels uncomfortable. Dialogue with her regularly, and advise her to come to you regularly with any questions or concerns that she may have about your relationship with him or her relationship with him. Teach her about inappropriate touching, how to say no, and how to speak up if it ever does happen. It is needless to say that, in the early stages of dating, this new man should never be left alone with her.

Speak up, Child, today, and save yourself from a paranoia tomorrow that may cause you to lose healthy male friendships and, even more, a healthy marriage.

Speak up, Child, and be saved.

Saved from Losing Credibility

When a crime of any kind is committed, the sooner it is reported, the more likely the chance of a favorable prosecution. When a crime is reported quickly:

- The victim's memory is fresher and can more easily recall the details of the incident.
- Any evidence that may have been left at the scene will be untainted.
- Any physical injuries sustained will be strong evidence against the perpetrator, as well as any physical injuries that he may have sustained as well.
- Credibility is key. It is key because family members, friends, and law enforcement personnel are more apt to believe someone

who comes to them in a frantic, a visibly distraught, and even more, a physically bruised state.

When a woman or a child shows up at a police station and claims she has just been molested or raped, she is treated as a priority, and it becomes rushed:

- She is rushed in to get medical attention, to be tested for sexually transmitted diseases and obtain any physical evidence left by the perpetrator.
- If she is underage, the parents are notified immediately and urged to rush down to the station.
- A unit is immediately dispatched to the perpetrator's location to bring him in for questioning.

However, when a twenty-four-year-old walks into a police station and says she was molested nineteen years ago, she is told to sit down and have a seat, and someone will get to her. Why is this? It is because her case is not as much of a priority as it would have been if she would have reported it immediately.

The delay in reporting makes a favorable prosecution now less likely. The delay in reporting makes the victim's memory of the events not as fresh. The delay in reporting has tainted all physical evidence. The delay in reporting has healed all or most physical injuries. The delay in reporting has, in some cases, painted a cloud over the victim's credibility. This is how it may be when you go to law enforcement for help for a crime that was committed decades ago.

However, even if you go to a family member and tell that person that another family member or household figure abused you nineteen years ago, your news will be received with, "Whaaaat?" Now this is not going to be a jubilant "whaaaat" by any means. It may be followed with the following:

- "Are you kidding?"
- "And you are just now telling us?"
- "I don't believe that sh*t!"
- "Then, if this is true, why didn't you tell us this before?"

- I knew it! And I asked you before, and you said no."
- "Well, what the hell are we supposed to do about it now?"

It is bad enough that you had to build up the courage to finally share this story that traumatically affected you for years, but then to be received with such disparaging remarks would just bring further humiliation to the situation.

Why should you be denied justice because you waited for a long time before you finally reported it? Why should you be denied justice because there is no longer any evidence left to support your story? Why should you be denied justice because your loved ones don't want to deal with it, nor do they want to deal with you?

Speak up, Child, and be saved.

Saved from Losing Faith

———— ⌖ ————

For those of us who are Christians, we usually dig down deep with praying when we have to go through a crisis. When a child is molested, this incident is her crisis.

When the attack occurred, she will have prayed for it to stop, but God did not answer that prayer as she had wished. When the attack was over, she will have prayed that it had never occurred, but God did not answer that prayer as she had wished. As time goes on and the attack is still fresh to her, she will pray that it just goes away, but God will not simply answer that prayer as well.

She will start to question God. Where were You? Why did You not help me? Do You not love me? Or, did You not help me because You are not real after all?

As the years go by and she continues to hold the occurrence of this event to herself, she will continue to find herself not at peace. In other words, this event, or this series of events, will haunt her for many years to come. Throughout all this, she will continue to pray for peace, and she may receive peace, but it will be a peace that comes and goes.

Will this child growing into a young lady find herself angry with God for allowing this to happen? Will this child growing into a young lady find herself not wanting to go to church anymore, that is, if she was going in the first place? Will this child growing into a young lady find herself totally losing her faith in God altogether?

Of course she can. She may lose her faith because she never found the peace that she was praying for. However, in order to receive that peace, in some cases, God may have been requiring an action on her part.

One action that may have been required is forgiveness. God may have wanted her to forgive her perpetrator. As hard as it may be for many to believe, God requires forgiveness, even in this case.

Now, this is not the type of forgiveness that is followed by just forgetting the whole thing ever happened. That would be ludicrous. It would be hard to trust in a God that demanded such from us, especially in this case. This would be the type of forgiveness that would be followed by an act of righteousness, an act of decency, or an act of justice.

But what if there is no righteousness? What if there is no decency? What if there is no justice? Then, does she have an obligation to forgive? The answer is yes.

"For if you forgive other people when they sin against you, your heavenly Father will also forgive you. But if you do not forgive others their sins, your Father will not forgive you your sins" (Matthew 6:15-15).

God wants you to forgive this man. Forgive this man in your heart, because he does not know what he has done, nor does he know what he will endure for what he has done.

God wants you to forgive this man. Forgive this man, so He can release the heavy burden that you are carrying on your shoulders and make it light. The heavy burden of hate, anger, revenge, mistrust, solitude, and suicide.

God wants you to forgive this man. Forgive this man, so He can begin to work on healing you emotionally, psychologically, physically, and spiritually.

You may not have felt God working on your behalf when this evil crime was committed. However, if you meet God halfway and do the extraordinary by forgiving this man, I can assure you that you will see Him moving in a powerful way when He moves in your life to restore you to a good state.

God wants you to forgive this man. Forgive this man, so you do not sin in your anger and bring more harm into your life.

God wants you to forgive this man. Forgive this man, so that you can live. He wants you to live a life that is fulfilling and joyous. He does not want you to live in the past, in the past of this evil event that occurred and be absorbed, stuck, and unable to move on.

God wants you to forgive this man. Forgive this man, so you will be of sound mind and at peace. God wants you to be these things so that when you speak up, you will be clear, and you will be heard.

The child who cries out hysterically with a distorted story that is full of emotion but lacks key, necessary details will be heard, but her story may not be quickly understood or received.

Forgive him, Child. Speak up, and be saved.

Saved from Becoming a Different Person

---⟨∽⟩---

Some of the sweetest little girls in the world have unfortunately become victims to evil, perverted men.

These sweet little girls smiled all the time. These sweet little girls laughed all of the time. They were picked up all of the time by family and friends because of how cute and joyful they were.

But then something happened. An event happened that changed this young girl's life. She was sexually molested. She was raped. She lost her innocence.

The girl no longer smiles. She no longer laughs. She no longer wants to be picked up by anyone except for that one person she still believes can protect her, whether it is her mother or father, but something has happened, so she has changed.

31

Now, she just stares. It is a deep, cold stare, as if she is still in shock. It looks as if she is still in shock, because she is. She is in shock because she has been violated. She is in shock because she knows that what happened should not have happened. She is in shock because she feels that someone has let her down, and it may be the sole person she wants to be picked up by.

Whether the child is three or ten, the story is the same. The child has lost her joy. The child has lost her joy because something has happened to her. One day, that person will go through hell for what he has done. But right now, the child is going through hell, a silent hell.

She wants to speak, but she doesn't know what to say. She wants to speak, but she does not know who to speak to. She wants to speak, but she is scared. She is scared about the consequences she may face when she does speak. She is scared and does not know if she is to just accept what was happened and move on or not.

What is she to move on to? Is she going to move on to this event happening again? It can be if this man is still around. Then, what the hell does she have to smile and laugh about? She should be in shock. She should be afraid. She should just stare. She should just stare and be on the lookout. She should be on the lookout for this man that has violated her.

This should not be. This should not be happening. No child should be on the lookout for an evil man who dwells within her midst. No child should lose her joy, lose her smile, and lose her ability to laugh because she is anticipating being raped by a man who has gained access into her life.

Child, do not allow this event to determine who you are going to be the rest of your life. You were once called "the happy baby." You were the child that everyone wanted to pick up and kiss all over the cheeks. You were the child who everyone wished were their own. You need to be that child again.

Child, do not allow this evil, perverted man to have this type of control over your life.

Child, do not allow this man to come into your bedroom one more night.

Child, do not allow this man to have the opportunity to threaten you or your parents again if you were to speak up.

Child, do not allow this man to come near you again with his dirty, sweaty, disgusting body.

Get mad. Get angry. Speak up, and be saved.

Saved from Missing the Window

————— ❧ —————

L ife is short. There are things we may want to do in life, but unfortunately, we may no longer be able to do some of those things because we missed the window.

Unfortunately, if you are a victim of a sexual predator and you do not report him within a reasonable amount of time, you may miss the window.

The statute of limitation for reporting this crime varies in each state, and depending on the state you live in, you may not have much time left, or you may have already missed the window.

If you allow this window to go by without acting upon it, you will not see justice be served. If justice is not served upon this man, you also will not have justice, nor will you have peace or the victory.

There will not be any exceptions in your case due to special circumstances. There will be no "your day in court," when you will be able to see this man for the last time and hear the judge ask the perpetrator, "Do you have any last words before I announce sentence?" which is followed by the perpetrator giving the standard and fake apology to you and your family before he is carried away in handcuffs to serve his time. There will be no sense of relief knowing this man will never be able to touch you or anyone else like this again because he will be finally behind bars because of what he has done.

Instead, there will only be a life of regrets because you missed the window. Instead, there will only be a case with no justice, no peace, and no victory. Instead, there will only be innocence lost, but no justice found.

This man deserves to be in prison for what he has done, but if you miss the window to report, then the only one that will be in prison is you. You will be locked up in the prison of your mind, and this prison will be hard to escape from. In this prison, you will keep reenacting the crime that was committed against you in your mind. Just as prison inmates are denied the beauty of the sun, you will be denied the beauty of joy, peace, freedom, and justice. This is the prison in which the innocent (yourself) is locked up, and the guilty (the perpetrator) has eluded imprisonment.

If you do not speak up and report this man to the authorities, you will allow this man to walk away a free man to enjoy life while you are left suffering, thinking forever of that dreadful night or period in which this man sexually assaulted you.

Speak up, Child, and be saved.

Saved from
Losing All Power

———⟨◦⟩———

When a child is in the midst of being sexually molested, the child may have lost her physical power to continue to fight back. However, when this vicious act is done, the child will have to speak up. If she does not, she may lose her power to say no in the future.

As unfortunate as it is, there may be more. There may be more men who may try to push themselves onto you sexually. They may not be like the monster who sexually assaulted you; this new man may be someone you are dating who may just want to go all the way with you one night because he believes that you got to that level of your relationship. However, if you have not brought closure to the horrible incident that occurred, and you are still haunted by it, then the same feeling you endured when that monster attacked you may arise and overwhelm you when your boyfriend or date decides to push himself upon you.

It is extremely important that you bury and bring closure to the incident that happened to you at the hands of this monster, and the only proper way of doing that is by speaking up and reporting him. Only then will you be able to distinguish the difference between what this monster did to you and what this new man is trying to do with you.

Wrong is wrong, and every man should listen when you say no, but the difference here is relationship.

The monster who imposed himself on you did not have a relationship with you that had the potential to lead to intimacy, especially in your eyes. However, your boyfriend, or this new man you are dating, does have a relationship with you that has the potential to lead to intimacy. His timing of when he thinks that the two of you are ready for intimacy may differ from yours; however, this is something that can be established with proper communication.

However, if you don't bring closure to what the monster did to you by speaking up and exposing him, then it is possible that when your boyfriend or this new man you are dating tries to take it to the next level by feeling you up and touching you in places that he has not touched you at before, then you may immediately see him as a monster, or even the monster.

If you do not speak up and expose the monster who attacked you, then when you are having an intimate moment with your boyfriend, you may also begin to relive the horrible incident that occurred in your head. This would then be followed up with you possibly freaking out and fighting your boyfriend as if he was the monster who sexually assaulted you. This would be unfortunate, especially if you also desire intimacy with your boyfriend, because your reaction may freak him out to the point that he runs away, not just physically but also from the relationship.

If you do not speak up and expose the monster who assaulted you, then you may also lose your power to continue to fight after you have said no.

When you were originally assaulted, you may have tried to fight off the monster who committed this horrible crime against you. You may have fought him off as hard as you could and even continued to say no, but at a certain point, you may have stopped fighting and stopped saying no because you became too weak to do anything further. That being the case, if you do not bring this incident to closure, in the future, when any man decides to press you into doing something more intimate than what desire to do, then you may subconsciously become prone to give up fighting and saying no because doing so failed you once before.

Do not allow this monster to take away all of your power. Do not allow this monster to take away the power to fight back. Do not allow this monster to take away your ability to distinguish the difference between what he did to you and what a man desiring your love wants to do with you. Do not allow this monster to take away your ability to continue to say no after you have clearly said no.

Speak up, Child, and be saved from losing all power.

Saved from Suicide

———— ❧ ————

When a child is first sexually assaulted, especially a child who does not report it, she wants it to just go away. However, she starts to realize that it is just not that easy. Sometimes, the attacks continue to happen, especially if the perpetrator lives in the same household. When she realizes that the memory of this is not going away, or worse, the perpetrator is not going away, she wants to go away. When going away is not an option, she may want to go away for good to get away from the pain and finally find peace by killing herself.

I know that it hurts. I know you are scared. I know everything seems dark, and you are consumed with grief that is pulling you in a direction that makes you want to put an end to it all. However, this is not the end that you should settle for, because this end will give the perpetrator an easy out.

He will get an easy out because he will walk away "scot free." He will walk away free because even though he had built up enough courage within himself to commit this evil deed, fear was running through this man after the crime was committed, fear of being exposed and punished. But with the you gone, his fear is gone, and he will be able to wipe the sweat away from his brows and move on with his life while you allowed him to take away yours.

Is this what you want? Is this how you want it to end? Is this how you want to be remembered? Or even yet, is this what you deserve?

Do you deserve to die because this man violated you? Do you deserve to die because he may have left you feeling ashamed? Do you deserve to die because he left you feeling angry, hurt, and scared? No? Then why do this to yourself?

Do your family and loved ones deserve to be left behind crying for answers? Do your family and loved ones deserve to be left behind wondering how they failed you? Do your family and loved ones deserve to be left behind with grief over your death that drives them close to death? No? Then why do this to them?

Does this man deserve to be left behind to be able to walk away scot free? Does this man deserve to be left behind to look for a new victim and deceive the loved ones in his life? Does this man deserve to be left behind to be able to prosper in life while your body wastes away in a cold tomb? No? Then why do this to him?

You do not deserve to die, and on the contrary, neither does this man. This would be too easy and would give him an easy out. This man deserves to sit in a prison cell and live with the same fear he made you feel. He will endure true fear because he will now be in the company of men who would love to beat him up and possibly rape him for his trespass against you. It is a true fear that may lead him to consider taking his own life. Now, of course, this is not what we would pray happens to him, but this just may happen, and it would be an ending that was paved because of the choices he made.

However, his ending should not be of any concern to you after you speak up and report him, and he is then convicted. He would then be at God's mercy, and God is just.

It is your ending that we are concerned with. This should not be your ending; his crime should not be the reason you take your own life.

It should instead end with life, a victorious life—a victorious life knowing that you overcame what happened to you and are victorious in putting this monster in prison.

It should instead end with success, a successful life with you being successful in your future career.

It should end with a fruitful life, a life that is fruitful in all your future endeavors, including raising a family, giving back to society, and touching other people's lives.

They say the best revenge is to show them that your life is getting better after they're gone. So, while this monster is gone, rotting in jail, and being punished for what he did, you are to move on with your life and become a success story. Therefore, don't give up on life, and instead live and be everything that you ever wanted to be before this horrific event occurred.

Speak up, Child, and be saved.

Saved from Accepting the Darkness

————— ❦ —————

When a child is raped, from the time the incident occurred to moments after, including the days and weeks to follow, it will be dark times, and what she does following the rape will determine if she will have days filled with light or days filled with darkness.

If you do not report this man for what he did, your days following the rape will be filled with darkness. They will be filled with grief, fear, sorrow, emotional and physical pain, thoughts of hurting yourself and or hurting someone else.

When you walk in this darkness, it will eventually be followed by defeat. You will be consumed by a feeling of defeat that will eat at your very soul. This feeling of defeat will have you believe that there is nothing that you can do to change your current situation. You will think that this is just how life is and that you just have to deal with it.

Moreover, you may be a child who is walking through life accepting what happened to you, or even worse, you may be a child who is walking through life accepting what is still happening to you.

If you have learned to accept what is still happening to you by this man and have accepted this as part of life, then you have crossed over to embracing the darkness.

When you accept something, you willingly support whatever it is. If you are actively being sexually assaulted by this man and are not doing anything to change the situation, you are embracing the darkness.

When you accept the darkness as a victim of sexual assault, you have accepted that this man has power over you to do with you what he wants. He may have even started having you appear at his place at his demand. He may have even started calling you every dirty name under the sun as he assaults you. He may have even started experimenting new sexual acts on you, all because you have accepted the darkness.

It would be horrible if you are actively going to school and are in a position to report this man but do not, for whatever reason. But, then you are going back to this man's house after school at his demand, so he can continue to rape you. It would be horrible if you are home with your parents every night, where you are in a position to report this man to your parents but do not, for whatever reason. Instead, this man is regularly picking you up after school so that he can continue to sexually assault you then drop you off at home. It would be horrible if it has gotten to the point that when your parents ask you, "How was your day?" you respond with, "It was fine." If these things are occurring, then you have accepted the darkness.

This man may be threatening you. You may even feel that you don't know if anyone is going to believe you at this point. You may even feel that you were brainwashed into going along with what this man was doing.

However, what has occurred and may even continue to occur is horrible, and it is wrong. It is something you must get yourself out of. No matter how long it has been going on, it is not too late to say, "No more," and take back your life.

Child, come out of the darkness, and come into the light. For in the light, there are many who are ready and willing to help you. They are ready to help you get the peace and stability in your life that you need. They are ready to help you get out of this sexually-abusive relationship. They are ready to help you prosecute this monster and put him in jail. They are ready to help you come out of the darkness.

Speak up, Child, and be saved.

Saved from Looking Like the Darkness

There is darkness all around us. Terrorism continues to grow and become more violent throughout the world. The list of active shooters continues to grow. And more sexual predators continue to come out of the cracks.

The individuals that partake in these crimes are evil, and there is no room for them in a civilized society. These individuals are so filled with darkness that eventually their evil desires had to come to the surface and become unleashed.

Unfortunately, besides these individuals who have committed these crimes, there are many others walking around who are filled with the same darkness. They may never go out and commit the same crimes, but the thirst to see these crimes unfold may haunt them. If you were a victim of being sexually assaulted as a child, and you have not brought closure to this matter, if you have not found peace in this matter, if you have never received any justice in this matter, then you may eventually look like the darkness.

No one can read your mind and know what you are thinking. No one can see what's going on in your heart. It is also possible that you may not know what is going on inside of your subconscious, for you may be deceived into thinking that you are alright and that this is no longer bothering you, but meanwhile, you may have become so hardened and callous that because of the evil that occurred to you, subconsciously, you may actually get a sense of comfort if this were to also occur to someone that you know.

Now, what happened to you is horrible and shouldn't even be wished on your worst enemy. And the chances of you being at peace with this happening to a friend or even your worst enemy is highly unlikely. That is, if you are emotionally healthy and stable, then you won't.

However, if you are not emotionally healthy and stable, because of what happened to you, then the years of not receiving the help you needed regarding the negative emotions you had to battle, including thoughts of taking your life, may have turned into dark thoughts. The dreaded darkness that you despised, the thought of a young girl being held against her will and being sexually assaulted by a dirty perverted man, is now the same darkness that you would be comfortable with if you found out it happened to someone else.

How could this have happened? How could you have become so callous and cold? Is it because of company? For it is said that misery loves company. I also believe it should be said that pain loves company.

When you first went through your pain, you found yourself all alone with no one to share it with you, but this was because no one knew what you were going through. Now that years have gone by, and you are still hurting emotionally and still longing for peace, there may not be anything more therapeutic for you than to have someone to talk to, someone, of course, that cannot only sympathize with you, but also empathize with you. However, if no such person is there that fits this description, then, when that day comes, and even if the abuse happened to one of your closest friends, when she reveals it to you, on the outside you may appear to be sympathetic, which, of course, will be genuine, but on the inside, something else may be going on. You may subconsciously have a slight sense of relief, because now you will no longer be alone in this matter.

Once again, how did this happen? How could you have gotten so callous and cold? It is because the darkness that attacked you has been allowed to linger in you for years and alter your way of thinking.

The darkness that hurt your way of thinking caused you to react differently. Instead of first thinking, *My poor friend. This happened to her too*, you may think, *Now, she will be able to relate to me.* Instead of first screaming out frantically, "Who the hell did this? What happened to my child? Someone call the police!" after finding out that your child may have been sexually assaulted, you now silently say to yourself, "Poor baby, I went through this and survived. You will too."

For those who know you, they may still see the sweet child in you they have always seen. But on the inside, only God can see the darkness that has been allowed to continue to build up inside of you.

Do not allow yourself to become hardened and callous on the inside like the monster who took advantage of you. Do not allow the same darkness to roam inside of you as that of the man who assaulted you.

Speak up, Child, and be saved.

Saved from Not Protecting Your Siblings

———⟨❧⟩———

There was a man who has been allowed to come into your home. This man may have been allowed in by your mother; maybe he is her new boyfriend. This man may have access to the home; maybe he is a family member. This man may see you on a regular basis; maybe he works at the school, the local store, or even at the church.

This man knows you. He knows you by name. He knows your family, your parents, and your siblings. He also knows how he was able to get away with what he did to you. Now, it is possible that he may try to see what he can get away with and do the same thing to your little sister.

The way that he buttered you up to make you trust him, he will do the same to your little sister. The gifts that he bought you to deceive you to believe that he cared for you, he will do the same to your little sister. The way that he laid on you the first time and said that it will not hurt (but it did), he will do the same to your little sister. The way that he threatened you or threatened to harm your parents if you squealed on him, he will do the same to your little sister. The way that he repeatedly violated and raped you, he will do the same to your little sister.

The panic you had to endure when this man first attacked you, your little sister will now have to feel it. The emotional and physical pain that you had to feel, your little sister will now have to feel it. The anxiety and pain that you had to feel every time you saw this man after the attack, your little sister will now have to feel it. The shame, confusion, anxiety attacks, and suicidal thoughts you face daily, your little sister will now have to feel it.

Is this fair? Is it fair that your little sister will have to go through this pain because of this evil man? Is it fair that your little sister will have to go through all of these emotional thoughts including suicide (and there is no guarantee that she will be as strong as you and not take her own life)? Is it fair that your little sister will go through all of this — and, when you think about it, may not have had to, if only her bigger sister would have spoken up and exposed this man?

If you are a bigger sister, it is your job to protect your little sister from this man. If you are a bigger sister, it is your job to show your little sister the right thing to do.

Speaking up and exposing this man is the right thing to do. Speaking up and exposing this man will save your little sister from having to deal with the same pain that you had to endure. Speaking up and exposing this man will save your little sister from committing suicide because of what this man did to her.

Speak up, Child, and be saved.

Saved from No One
Caring Anymore

———————— ❦ ————————

Everyone loved you when you were a child. You were so adorable and fun to play with. Then, as you got older, your demeanor changed, especially after what the monster did to you.

When your demeanor changed, it would have been noticeable. That being the case, those close to you would have, or should have, been asking about the reason for the change.

However, as time went on, and there were no definitive answers as to why there was any change, people moved on.

Those who inquired about what happened to you at the time moved on. They moved on in life. Changes in their own lives made whatever happened to you fade into the background. For some of them, the girl that they see today is not the same loving child they cared for and loved before. Instead, you became just another child they see every now and then.

Let's fast forward to the day and year when you finally came forward and spoke up. Let's look at some of those people who were first inquiring about what happened to you during that period — some were family, and some were friends. However, some of them are probably not in your life anymore. Some of them probably don't even remember your name anymore; they remember you as that cute little girl who changed. Once, they called you by your name. Now you are known only as the daughter of ...

Now they hear about what happened to you years ago, and, of course, they will all have different responses. The closer family members would — or should — come to your side immediately to support you, unless one of them was the predator, which, of course, will change the whole dynamic of the situation.

However, let's look at everyone else. Let's look at the family members who were not that close and the friends who were around at the time. How do they respond to this?

Some may call your parents immediately and tell them they will be there for them, whatever they may need. Some may not even call and only discuss amongst themselves whether the story is true or not. Some, unfortunately, may not care anymore. This is not because they don't care about you as a person, but because they have moved on with their lives.

Now, my question for you is, how does this make you feel? How does it make you feel to know that all these people that you had in your life at one time that would have done pretty much anything for you, now don't really care enough to get involved?

The saying goes, "It takes a village to raise a child." This is true for many reasons. However, it also applies in a village that is plagued by a sexual assault.

When a child is sexually molested, the village (or community of loved ones), will provide comfort and console the victim and the family of the victim. The village will provide security for the victim and make certain that the perpetrator will not have access to the victim again. The village will give the victim and the family the best avenues of approach to handle the matter, which is important, because the victim and the family may not be thinking rationally. The village can help with other household work that needs to be done, such as cleaning, food shopping, running errands, or there may be other young kids who need to be taken to school or may need a babysitter. And one of the most important things that the village can do for you is just be there.

If you are a victim of sexual abuse, do not take for granted the village that God has allowed to be in your life and the things that they can do for you, including the things mentioned above and many more, because you may eventually lose them. You may lose them to life because life may move them around and plant them in new villages. And as members of new villages, when they hear about what happened to you, they will be concerned, but not enough to take up arms for you simply because they have their own village to worry about. So unfortunately, you will be lucky if you even hear from some of them.

Take advantage of the village in your life, those who are there to love and protect you. Take advantage of the village in your life, those who ready to hear you speak up, so they can take up arms for you and see to it that you are saved.

Speak up, Child, and be saved.

Saved from Fighting Back Yourself

———————— ❧ ————————

It may not happen the day of the attack. It may not happen the day after. It may not even happen a year later, but there will come a day in which you may want to fight back. You may want to go after this man or have someone else do it on your behalf. You may want to see him physically injured. You may want some guys you know to go after him and beat him down. You may even want to get hold of a gun yourself so you can shoot him. These feelings will come, but you must be saved from them.

You must be saved from these feelings because they will only bring about your own destruction. Not only will you face the legal ramifications of your act, but you will also be consumed by the darkness.

The darkness will cause you to become obsessed with having this man hurt and bringing pain to him. The darkness will cause you to become obsessed with possibly stalking this man, to find out his every whereabouts as you plan your attack. The darkness may cause you to switch roles with this man; now you become the hunter, and he becomes the prey. The darkness may even have you in a position where your prey has been caught, and you are now torturing him.

Where would the justice be if after all you have endured at the hands of this man, you are now the one in front of a judge to answer for what you have done? Where would the justice be if after this man took away your innocence, now your freedom is taken away because of what you did? Where would be the justice be if there is no legal justice against this man?

For every action, there is a reaction. If your reaction to this man's action is fighting back, then you will have allowed this man to win in the long run. He won because besides taking away your innocence, he took away your free life.

He took away your life of peace. A peaceful life that includes getting married and having a beautiful family. A life of raising your own beautiful children, getting a house with your family, having a career, and he took away your life of being successful and productive in today's society. He took away your freedom, because you decided to fight back yourself and did not give the justice system the opportunity to work on your behalf. Instead, you are sitting in a prison cell wondering how you got there.

You deserve to live and have a life that is full of joy, peace, and fun. However, if you allow yourself to be consumed with fighting back yourself, then you have allowed this man to continue to be the pinnacle of your very existence.

Speak up, Child, and be saved.

Saved from the
Vicious Cycle

It is said that history repeats itself. If you were a victim of sexual abuse, you certainly do not want this saying to become reality in your family. If this saying does become a reality in your family, and unfortunately it has for some sexual-abuse victims, then it would mean that as a victim, you will also become a sexual abuser of a child, possibly even your own.

There could be nothing more tragic than you, having endured harm by this man, to now go out and subject an innocent child to what you endured.

One of the reasons that some victims become predators themselves is because what happened to them was not an isolated attack. Instead, it was a prolonged series of attacks that unfortunately for some became a way of life.

Your continued abuse by this man might have lasted for weeks, months, and even—horrifically— for years. Even if it lasted only a few days, to a child, this could seem like a lifetime, a lifetime that no child should have to go through.

The reason this became a lifetime for you is because for a lifetime the images and thoughts of what happened to you continue to replay through your head, and without constructive therapy, these images and thoughts can become more and more powerful and destructive. These thoughts will become powerful enough to keep you entangled in the events that occurred, so powerful that it may seem like it is still happening. These thoughts will also become destructive enough to make you react, but unfortunately in a negative way. That negative way may be to become so callous as to inflict on a child who is looking at you with loving eyes humiliation, torture, and sexual abuse.

Do you remember the first time this man attacked you? Do you remember the feeling of shock and horror? Do you remember the physical pain that you endured, the unanswered cry for help, and then the long period that you just laid there and cried and cried?

Is this what you want another child to go through? Do you want an innocent child to look up at you with the look of, "Why are you doing this?" in her eyes? Do you want an innocent child to lay helplessly underneath you, screaming in pain, as you penetrate her with an object, an object that is causing her physical pain and may be also be doing permanent damage? Do you want to be in a position of forcing a child down on the bed while you are slapping her to try to get her to stop screaming for help?

Is this what you want another child to go through, especially at your hands?

End the cycle. Speak up, Child, and be saved.

Saved from a Life of Selling What was Taken from You

In many ways, sexual abuse hurts. It hurts a child physically, mentally, and emotionally. And when a child is hurt emotionally for a long period of time with no one to share it with, their judgment and rationale can become clouded. Examples of this could be picking the right boyfriend, or in some cases, just picking one boyfriend.

For some young girls, the devastation of being sexually molested has clouded their way of thinking to the point that they believe that being promiscuous is one way of dealing with and forgetting the pain that this monster caused them.

Now, of course, by being promiscuous, she has opened the door to other problems such as sexual diseases like HIV, chlamydia, etc. In addition, she will have low self-esteem, a bad reputation, and a callousness toward true or real love and intimacy.

If you have become promiscuous to try to forget what happened to you by this monster, then what you have done is created a temporary Band-Aid for your problem. However, this temporary Band-Aid has the potential of doing more harm than good. In cases where many different men know that you are promiscuous, many of them are not going to respect you, and will just see you as a piece of sex, and unless you are comfortable being viewed and considered a piece of meat, then you are being used by them. Now, of course, there may be one or two guys in that group that may claim to love you, but even some of those may fall in love with you because you are giving it up, and they may have not been getting sex from anyone else other than you during.

However, for those guys you are having sex with, those who you know deep down are just having fun, what is the possibility that they are having fun with others as well? And if so, are they having unprotected sex with them just like they are doing with you? And if so, how many of those men are knowingly walking around with something that is bringing discomfort to his private part, whether it is burning when he urinates, or something that is making him scratch all day, but he is scared to get it checked. Is this the risk that you are willing to take to try to forget the root of your problem, the problem that could have gone away if you had spoken up? Or what about the guy who has tested positive for HIV and then decides to keep it on the "down low"? Now what if that "down low" became public knowledge and the rumor is out there that he has HIV? Do you know the anxiety and the worry that you will go through you when you pace back and forth wondering if you caught it from him? What happens if you do catch it from him?

How are you going to tell your parents and loved ones, or will you tell them? After the initial shock has gone away of finding out that you have been exposed, will you continue to sleep around and be promiscuous? And no matter what you decide to do at that point, will it all have been worth it?

Some young women who have become promiscuous eventually felt, "Why should I give it away for free, when I can make money for it?"

Some of these women may entice some of the men they date to award them with gifts as compensation for having sex with them. However, some of these women have become prostitutes.

It is a tragedy when a young girl is sexually abused, but it becomes another tragedy when that child continues to struggle with the direction of her life because of what occurred to her and then becomes a prostitute.

There is no denying the horrors that prostitutes must face on a daily basis: exposure to sexual diseases; physical abuse by men; criminal prosecution, depression and despair, being held against her will, just to mention a few.

Whether you are having guys buy you gifts because they get to have sex with you, or you are walking the streets selling your body, you have allowed one tragedy to spiral into another.

Why would you do this? These men do not love you, and in most cases, they do not even care about you. They care about having sex just with your body, because many of these men may not even see your face while they are having sex with you because they just may be imagining that you are someone else, such as their wives.

How deplorable is this? You are giving to this man what is supposed to be precious of yours, and he doesn't even recognize your identity? Nor does he care to. You are giving to this man what is supposed to be precious of yours, and he lays there and demeans you by calling you derogatory names while you pleasure him. You are giving to this man what is supposed to be so precious of yours, and in return he fills you with his loaded weapon, a weapon that he knows is loaded with a STD, and yet he doesn't care if you were to become infected or not.

Why do you allow your life to continue to spiral down because of what this man has done to you? Why do you allow yourself to be degraded by dirty-minded men who do not care for you or your welfare? Why do you allow more men to take advantage of you, especially after what this monster did to you?

Speak up, Child, and be saved.

Saved from Suspecting Involvement by Loved Ones

I t is the responsibility of the parent to protect their children from things, or in this case, people who can cause them harm. It is the responsibility of the parent to protect their children from having to face the horrors that some young women had to endure that was mentioned in this book. However, and unfortunately, some parents not only fail to protect their children from being molested, but they also play a role in what occurred to them.

There are different levels of a parent's role in the sexual abuse of his or her own child. They are as follows:

- The parent plays a physical role in sexually abusing his child. In this case, the parent becomes the monster.

- The parent is aware of the sexual abuse that her child is enduring due to obvious signs and changes that her child is going through, but for some reason turns a blind eye.
- The parent is addressed by the child or someone else that something has happened to her daughter, however, adamantly refuses to believe that anything occurred. Therefore, the parent does not follow up on it or even question the alleged suspect. Worse even, in some cases, the mother will even call her daughter a liar.

My question, Child, is this: What role did your parent play in this, if any?

Did your father sexually abuse you? Did your father rape you repeatedly for years and was never held accountable for it? How is your relationship with your father now? Have you ever forgiven him? Is this act still going on?

In most cases, when a father is sexually abusing his daughter, the daughter does not want to expose her father because she does not wish for him to get in trouble and to go to jail because she still loves her father. However, she does want the abuse to stop. She does want for her life to be normal again (if it ever was), so that she can be innocent and play with kids her age and look up to her parents in a loving way as her providers and protectors. Instead, she must fear her father because he is hurting her and exposing her to adult behaviors because of his selfish and perverted desires.

The unfortunate truth is this: your father is a monster, and he should be in prison for what he has done to you.

What about your mother? Were you being sexually abused by a man, your father or one of your mother's lovers, and though she knew about it, she did nothing?

In a case where a man is sexually abusing his lover's daughter and the mother is aware and does not get involved, it is because of one of a couple of reasons:

- The mother has, for some reason, chosen her mate over her daughter and does not want to lose him no matter what evil he is doing.
- The mother was also sexually abused as a child, and instead of her working harder

to prevent her child from also becoming a victim, she believes that since she survived her ordeal, her child will survive as well.

- The mother may be allowing the daughter to be sexually abused by a man who is not her father as a way of getting back at the father for leaving her, especially in the case where the daughter was "daddy's little girl."

- The mother may be genuinely afraid of her mate to the point that she won't even protect her own daughter.

- The mother may have serious self-esteem issues and believes this is her only hope of a relationship, so she is willing to turn a blind eye to this situation.

No matter what her reasoning may be, if your mother participated in your violation in any of these levels, then your mother will also pay for her contribution. Unfortunately, she may not face a jury of her peers, but she will also be accountable to God for what she has done, or failed to do, and that is to come to your rescue.

What about your mother once again? Was it brought to her attention that something may be going on with you, and she refused to believe it, even if the claim came from you? Has she gone as far as calling you a liar, or has she stated that you are jealous of her relationship with this man in her life, the man that sexually abused you?

How does this make you feel, knowing that your own mother will call you a liar after you told her this man, who is residing in your house, has touched you? What do you do now that you have told your mother and she doesn't believe, and you still have to face this man and possibly still be alone in the house with him?

Then, you tell everyone else. You tell every relative you have. You tell all your friends' parents. You tell everyone in a position of authority at school. You go into a police station, a hospital, a church, and you speak up.

This may mean that you may be removed from your home. This may also mean that your parents may be investigated whether they were involved or not. However, these things must happen to get you help and to stop the abuse from occurring.

These things must also happen to get you answers, for these investigations will reveal the truth of who, in addition to the monster, was involved and to what level, so that you will not have to forever wonder and suspect those closest to you of being involved.

A child that is left to wonder if her mother knew that she was being raped by this man that she is no longer with will eat at her soul and will never give her rest. She will always distrust her mother, which may be one that is unjust.

Speak up, Child, and be saved.

The Aftermath of Speaking Up

───❧───

When you speak up, life is going to change. It is going to change for you and for the monster who disrupted your life.

Your life is going to change because you will begin to experience freedom, freedom of moving on from having to had to live with this burden in silence — this burden that has held you down, caused you pain, caused you isolation, and caused you fear. Now, you are free from those burdens, and regardless of the outcome of the legal proceedings, you will be free to move on, no matter what.

The life for the monster will change as well. He will not experience the freedom that you will experience. Instead, he will begin to experience justice being served on him.

This man will first experience the emotional trauma of knowing he has been exposed. This emotional trauma will go through his entire body, into his bones, and tear through his soul. Inside, this emotional trauma will be a strong fear that everyone will find out what he has done including his family, friends, and law enforcement.

If this man has moved on in life and is now married with children, he will now have to explain to them what he has done, unless he chooses to lie to beat the charges. He will now be filled with a strong fear because he knows that he may be confronted by people who will be angry and may want to retaliate with violence. Finally, this man will now be filled with a strong fear of knowing that it won't be long before a detective will knock on his door to ask him questions or arrest him.

From that point on, if this man is lucky enough to escape any street justice that might be administered by the family, then he will have to begin the fear of going through the legal process.

While you can begin to feel the weight of that burden that you were carrying around beginning to lift off you, this man will feel just the opposite:

- He will be constantly weighed down with the possibility of getting jail time for what he has done. In addition, every time he must make a court appearance or go in for questioning for any matter, fear and distress is going to tear at his soul.

- He will be in turmoil with his wife, as he will constantly explain to her that this is all a lie and that it never happened. This turmoil may even be filled with fighting and threats from her that if he is found guilty she will leave him and see to it that he will never see their kids again.

- If this man is found guilty, or perhaps even if he is placed into jail once he is arrested, then this man's job and/or career will be on the line when it is revealed, especially when the crime that he participated in is revealed. Most companies will probably fire him immediately, even prior to a conviction, if he was arrested for sexually assaulting a child.

This man's world will begin to fall apart—his family life, his finances, and his emotional stability.

As far as a conviction, there is no guarantee that he will go to jail even if he is convicted. It is possible that he may only have to register as a sexual offender with time served if he sat in jail upon first being picked up. It is even possible that the case may not even go that far because all the years that have passed since this crime occurred have made it hard to put together the necessary evidence.

Because of this, you may be somewhat apprehensive to come forward and finally speak up. However, remember that even though you will not be able to see what he is going through behind closed doors, this man will be hurting, and justifiably so.

Speak up, Child, and be saved.

Epilogue

————❦————

This book was written for the many women who have shared their stories with me. Each one of them pained me to hear, so much so that I wanted to act on your behalf. I wanted to find these evil men and instill the fear in them they instilled in every one of you when you were younger.

However, my desire would not have served the greater good. So, my prayer is that this book will reach the many others who are having to face what you have faced. The many others who are currently having to make serious life decisions regarding this matter.

My prayer is that every child out there who is a victim of this horrendous crime gets the justice that they deserve, along with the peace and healing they need to become victorious in life and to no longer have the stigma of being a victim hanging over their heads.

Speak up, Child, and be saved.

CPSIA information can be obtained
at www.ICGtesting.com
Printed in the USA
FSHW021140091118
53592FS